Green

Moira Anderson

www.raintreepublishers.co.uk
Visit our website to find out more information about **Raintree** books.

To order:
☎ Phone 44 (0) 1865 888112
▤ Send a fax to 44 (0) 1865 314091
🖥 Visit the Raintree Bookshop at **www.raintreepublishers.co.uk** to browse our catalogue and order online.

First published 2005 by Heinemann Library
a division of Harcourt Education Australia,
18–22 Salmon Street, Port Melbourne Victoria 3207
Australia (a division of Reed International Books Australia
Pty Ltd, ABN 70 001 002 357).
Visit the Heinemann Library website
www.heinemannlibrary.com.au

Published in Great Britain by Heinemann Library,
Halley Court, Jordan Hill, Oxford OX2 8EJ,
part of Harcourt Education
www.heinemann.co.uk/library

R A Reed Elsevier company

Editorial: Moira Anderson, Carmel Heron
Design: Sue Emerson (HL-US), Marta White
Photo research: Jes Senbergs, Wendy Duncan
Production: Tracey Jarrett

Typeset in 26/32 pt Infant Gill Regular
Film separations by Print + Publish, Port Melbourne
Printed and bound in China by
South China Printing Company Ltd.

The paper used to print this book comes from sustainable
resources.

**National Library of Australia
Cataloguing-in-Publication data:**
Anderson, Moira (Moira Helen).
    Green.

    Includes index.
    For lower primary school students.
    ISBN 1 74070 288 3.

    1. Colors – Juvenile literature. 2. Green – Juvenile
literature. I. Title. (Series : Read and learn).
(Series : Finding colours).

535.6

Acknowledgements
The publisher would like to thank the following for
permission to reproduce photographs: Rob Cruse
Photography: pp. **6, 8, 10, 11**; Corbis: pp. **22, 24**; Getty
Images: p. **16**; Getty Images/PhotoDisc: p. **15**, /National
Geographic/George Grall: pp. **20, 23**; PhotoDisc, pp. **4, 5,
7, 9, 12, 13, 14, 18, 19, 20, 21, 23** (all except frog feet);
photolibrary.com/Plainpicture: p. **17**.

Front cover photograph permission of Tudor Photography,
back cover photographs permission of Getty Images/
National Geographic/George Grall (frog) and PhotoDisc
(grapes).

Every attempt has been made to trace and acknowledge
copyright. Where an attempt has been unsuccessful, the
publisher would be pleased to hear from the copyright
owner so any omission or error can be rectified.

Contents

Some words are shown in bold, **like this**.
You can find them in the glossary on page 23.

What is green?

Green is a colour.

What different colours can you see in this picture?

The colour green is all around.

What green things can you see
in this picture?

What green things can I eat?

When green pears are soft,
we can eat them.

These grapes are green.

Grapes grow in bunches.

What other green food can I eat?

Green lettuce is good in a sandwich.

Lettuce is good in salads too.

These green beans are long
and crunchy.

Most people cook green beans
to eat them.

What green things are there at home?

This sofa is green.

It is soft and comfy to sit on.

This glass is green.

Glass is hard and smooth.

What is green in the garden?

blades

There is green grass in the garden.

The **blades** of grass are green.

These herbs are green.

Herbs are put in food to add **flavour**.

What else is green in the garden?

This hosepipe is green.

It is used to water the **plants**.

This watering can is green.

It is used to water the plants too.

Water helps the plants to grow.

What is green in the playground?

This roundabout is green.

It goes round and round.

This toy is green.

It goes backwards and forwards.

What green things grow?

stem

leaves

This **plant** grows
in a pot.

Its **leaves** and **stems** are green.

These green plants grow in the pond.

The big flat leaves float on top of the water.

Are there green animals?

This frog is green.

The **suckers** on its feet help it climb.

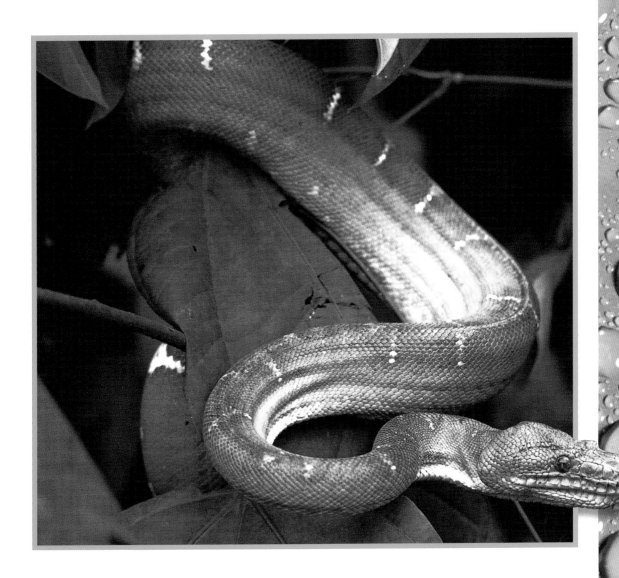

This snake is green.

It can be hard to see this snake
on green plants.

Quiz

What green things can you see?

Look for the answers on page 24.

Glossary

blades
flat, thin leaves

flavour
the taste of something you eat

leaves
flat parts of a plant that grow
from the stem

plant
a living thing that cannot move; most
need soil, water, and sun to grow

stems
parts of plants where the
flowers and leaves grow

suckers
sticky pads that hold on to things

Index

Answers to the quiz
on page 22

trees

T-shirt

grass

Notes to parents and teachers

Reading non-fiction texts for information is an important part of a child's literacy development. Readers can be encouraged to ask simple questions and then use the text to find the answers. Each chapter in this book begins with a question. Read the questions together. Look at the pictures. Talk about what the answer might be. Then read the text to find out if your predictions were correct. To develop readers' enquiry skills, encourage them to think of other questions they might ask about the topic. Discuss where you could find the answers. Assist children in using the contents page, picture glossary and index to practise research skills and new vocabulary.

Titles in the **Finding Colours** series include:

ISBN   1 74070 287 5

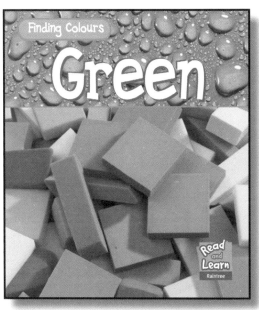

ISBN   1 74070 288 3

ISBN   1 74070 289 1

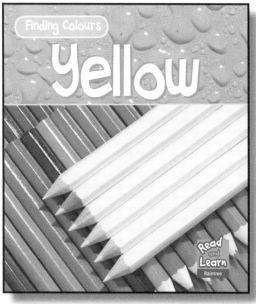

ISBN   1 74070 290 5

Find out about the other titles in this series on our website www.raintreepublishers.co.uk